# Understanding
# Citizenship 3

Second Edition

Tony Thorpe

**HODDER**
EDUCATION
PART OF HACHETTE LIVRE UK

INDIVIDUALS
ENGAGING IN
SOCIETY

CitizenshipFoundation

The Citizenship Foundation is an independent educational charity, which aims to help young people to engage in the wider community through education about the law, democracy and society. It produces the Young Citizen's Passport (also published by Hodder Education), which can be used in conjunction with this book.

For further details of the work and activities of the Citizenship Foundation see the Foundation's website at www.citizenshipfoundation.org.uk, or contact The Citizenship Foundation, 63 Gee Street, London EC1V 3RS.

Telephone: (44) 020 7566 4141. E-mail: info@citizenshipfoundation.org.uk

The Publishers would like to thank the following for permission to reproduce copyright illustrations in this book:
Ablestock, contents page, 6 (left & right), 8 (background), 11 (right top/heroin), 15 (heroin syringes), 17 (backgrounds, pizza & cake), 20 (DJ & image on TV), 21 (left & right), 35, 37 (background), 38 (middle & bottom centre), 47 (centre), 49 (all), 53 (left), 55, 60 (bottom), 64 (middle), 67; Corbis, 24, 46 (left); Council of Europe for the European Court of Human Rights photo, 64; Mary Evans, 40, contents page; Eyewire, 27, 38 (background); Getty Images, 58; Ingram Publishing for the photos of Flora, 54 and Hitler, 62; iStockphoto, contents page, 7 (all), 9, 11 (left, right middle & bottom), 15 (all except heroin & LSD), 16, 17 (tortilla & fizzy drink), 18, 20 (newspapers, magazines & TV), 22 (background), 27 (right background), 33, 34, 38 (3 figures bottom left & right), 39 (top left), 42-43, 44-45, 46 (top right), 47 (all passports except UK), 48, 53 (right), 59, 60 (middle & bottom), 61 (all), 64 (interrogation and evidence tape); Mirrorpix, 23; Andrew Murray/ Rex Features, 10; Nomad Graphique, 15 (heroin spoon), 20 (signs at Piccadilly circus), 28 (left), 30, 32 (right), 34, 64 (evidence bag); PA Photos, 14, 37 (bottom right); PA photos/ EPA/ Steffen Schmidt, 60 (top); PA Photos/ Ian Nicholson, contents page, 65; Photo Alto, 38 (top), 39 (centre & bottom); Photodisc, contents page, 8 (bottom), 25, 28 (right), 35, 47 (UK passport), 54 (all except Flora), 56 (bottom); Photofusion Picture Library/ Alamy, 50; Rex Features, 19, 26 (left), 41; Sipa Press/ Rex Features, contents page, 26 (right); SPL, 15 (LSD); ©Transport for London. The map on 32 (left) reproduced by kind permission of TfL.

The publishers would also like to thank the following for permission to reproduce material in this book:

ASH for Factsheet no. 1, smoking statistics, reproduced by permission of Action on Smoking and Health, page 6; ABC (Audit Bureau of Circulations) for 'Daily UK newspaper sales', reproduced by permission of Audit Bureau of Circulations, page 22; Aegis Trust for stories about "Elma", "Henry", "Howard" and "Peter" on pages 50, 51, 62-63; Crown copyright material is reproduced under Class Licence Number: CO2P0000060 with the permission of the Controller of HMSO, page 32; 'Results of questionnaire on drugs' from the British Crime Survey (2005-6) on page 11 and the image of the Race Relations Act 1976 on page 57.

Every effort has been made to establish copyright and contact copyright holders prior to publication. If contacted, the publisher will be pleased to rectify any omissions or errors at the earliest opportunity.

The author would like to thank Don Rowe and Jan Newton for their editorial advice and support, and Terry Fiehn, Rachel Gore, Ted Huddleston, Richard Jarvis, Dan Mace, and Jay Warner for their help in preparing and checking the text.

Every effort has been made to trace all copyright holders, but if any have been inadvertently overlooked the Publishers will be pleased to make the necessary arrangements at the first opportunity.

Although every effort has been made to ensure that website addresses are correct at time of going to press, Hodder Education cannot be held responsible for the content of any website mentioned in this book. It is sometimes possible to find a relocated web page by typing in the address of the home page for a website in the URL window of your browser.

Hachette's policy is to use papers that are natural, renewable and recyclable products and made from wood grown in sustainable forests. The logging and manufacturing processes are expected to conform to the environmental regulations of the country of origin.

Orders: please contact Bookpoint Ltd, 130 Milton Park, Abingdon, Oxon OX14 4SB. Telephone: (44) 01235 827720. Fax: (44) 01235 400454. Lines are open 9.00–5.00, Monday to Saturday, with a 24-hour message answering service. Visit our website at www.hoddereducation.co.uk

Copyright © The Citizenship Foundation 2005, 2008
First published in 2005 by
Hodder Education,
Part of Hachette Livre UK,
338 Euston Road,
London NW1 3BH

This second edition first published 2008

Impression number     5  4  3  2  1
Year                              2013  2012  2011  2010  2009  2008

Cover photo: ©moodboard/Alamy.
Design and Illustrations by Nomad Graphique.
Typeset in Garamond 3 15pt, Helvetica Neue 13pt.
Printed in Italy.

A catalogue record for this title is available from the British Library.

ISBN: 978 0340 959 206

# Contents

# Tobacco

In this unit we look at some of the effects of smoking and ask what action should be taken to discourage people from buying cigarettes and tobacco.

## Tricky business

Sophie is 13 years old. She walks through the door of a newsagent's. A woman of about 30 follows her into the shop. Sophie asks for 20 cigarettes and hands over a £10 note. The sales assistant takes the money and gives Sophie the cigarettes, along with her change.

Sophie leaves the shop alone. The woman introduces herself to the sales assistant. She explains that she is from the local trading standards department, and says that a girl of 13 has just been sold a packet of cigarettes.

Sophie wasn't buying the cigarettes for herself. She was helping in a campaign to catch shopkeepers who sell cigarettes to young people under 18.

The maximum fine for this offence is £2,500. It was the first time this shopkeeper had been caught. He was fined £350.

### ? Questions ? ? ? ? ? ?

**1** Sophie was helping to trap shopkeepers selling cigarettes to young people under 18. Is this a good idea? Is it fair? Give reasons for your answer.

**2** Look at the graph below. Try to make at least two observations about each group.

## Smoking trends

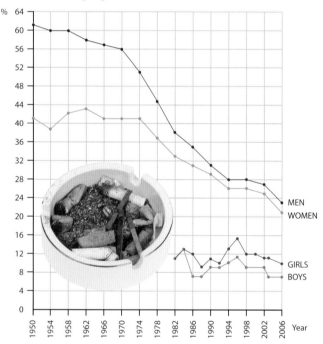

▼ 1950–2006, percentage of UK men and women smoking cigarettes.

MEN
WOMEN
GIRLS
BOYS

Percentage of regular smokers in England, aged 11-15 by sex: 1982-2006. ▲

## Costs

Tobacco is very addictive. Doctors believe it is the most serious form of drug addiction in Britain. About 1,000 people are admitted to hospital in Britain each day for diseases related to smoking. The cost of treatment is put at £1.5 billion a year.

An estimated 112,000 people in Britain die each year from tobacco-related illnesses. The charity Cancer Research estimates that six million people have died in Britain through smoking over the past 50 years.

## Second-hand smoke

Cigarettes also affect those who don't smoke. A mother who smokes while pregnant risks harming her unborn child. Children who live with smokers tend to have poorer health than those who do not.

A lot of second-hand smoke simply burns from the end of a cigarette, and because it hasn't been filtered it can be more dangerous than the smoke inhaled by smokers themselves.

# The law

### Sales

In October 2007 it became illegal to sell tobacco products to anyone under 18. Shopkeepers or sales assistants who sell cigarettes to anyone under 18 commit a criminal offence and may be prosecuted and fined.

### Advertising

The Tobacco Advertising and Promotion Act 2002 forbids the advertising of all tobacco products – including sports sponsorship.

### In public

Smoking in enclosed public places has been banned throughout the UK since July 2007.

**3** Here are some ways of reducing the harm caused by cigarettes and tobacco, particularly to young people.

- Ban the sale of cigarettes and tobacco.
- Allow the sale – but not permit the display of cigarettes.
- Increase the size of health warnings on packets.
- Double the price of cigarettes by increasing the tax charged on each packet.
- Ban the sale of packs of ten cigarettes.
- Require anyone who sells cigarettes to have a licence.

**a** Would you reject any of these ideas straightaway? Explain why.

**b** If you could only choose three proposals, which would you select, and why?

**c** Are there any further ideas of your own that you would like to add?

**4** Some people say that the ban on smoking, particularly in pubs, is unfair. What are the arguments for and against this idea?

◄ You can't buy cigarettes until you are 21 in Japan.

▲ Smoking has been banned in almost all public places in Britain since 2007.

# Alcohol

## Legal substance

There's a drug on the market that is linked to more than 40,000 deaths in Britain every year, and lands more than 150,000 people in hospital through accidents and illness. Each year it costs the National Health Service more than £3 billion in treatment and care.

The drug is a significant cause of accidents at work. It greatly contributes to street crime, and thousands of serious assaults and murders have been committed under its influence. One overseas dealer working in Britain and selling the drug made £900 million in the last seven years.

This substance is alcohol. The overseas dealer is an international company that has, amongst its investments, 7,000 British pubs.

It is not all bad news, however. The drinks industry in Britain provides about a million jobs, and brings in about £7 billion in taxes.

## Doctors' orders

Most people in Britain, for most of the time, don't have a problem with alcohol. Scientific research has shown that moderate drinking, for older people in particular, has some health benefits.

Government safe drinking levels recommend a maximum limit of 14 units of alcohol per week for women and 21 units per week for men. (1 unit = $^1/2$ pint of beer, a small glass of wine or a single measure of spirits.)

However, too much alcohol damages many organs in the body, causing problems such as high blood pressure and disease of the liver – a vital organ in the body. Chronic liver disease in Britain has doubled over the past 20 years.

## Dying for a drink

**Julia, 23, lives and works in Leeds. Five nights a week she goes to a bar or pub.**

'I probably drink about ten pints a week, plus wine with meals in the evening and a few alcopops and cocktails on Saturday night. All my friends drink, and today it's OK for women to drink as much as men. I have quite a stressful job, and I go out drinking to relax and be with my friends.

Drinking is a good way to switch off. I feel sorry for people who don't drink. They miss out on such a lot. Having a drink is the best way to get to know someone.'

## ? Questions

1 Is there anything that Julia says that you disagree with? If so, what is it, and why?

2 Is Julia taking any risks? If so, what are they?

# The weekend starts here

Each night, from Thursday until Saturday, the centres of many towns and cities throughout Britain are full of thousands of people moving between bars, pubs and clubs.

This is not a new feature of life in Britain, but heavy drinking is on the increase and Britain has a reputation of having one of the worst binge-drinking problems in Europe.

Drunkenness, violence and anti-social behaviour are common in many town and city centres at night, with crimes being committed that would not even be attempted during the daytime.

▲ One police officer said recently, 'If you took away alcohol from a town centre, there would be no disorder.'

## A changing climate

Many new bars have opened in recent years. Old buildings – particularly banks – are now used for entertainment. Today, people drink outside the bar, on the street – something that was almost unknown in Britain until a few years ago.

Recent changes to the licensing laws allow many pubs and bars to stay open all day. In the past, they opened only in the evening, mainly from 7p.m. until 10.30p.m., and for a brief period at lunchtime. Many bars and pubs also offer a 'happy hour' during the early evening, when drinks are available cheaply.

## The law

**Buying and selling alcohol**

It is an offence to sell alcohol to anyone under 18 – unless it can be shown that the landlord or bar staff did their best to check the person was 18 or over. It is an offence to sell alcohol to someone who looks as if they have already had too much to drink.

**Drinking in public**

Some local councils have banned the drinking of alcohol in public. The police also have the power to order people not to drink alcohol in public and can take away alcohol from anyone under 18 who is drinking in public.

3   The police suggest banning the sale of alcohol at night in town and city centres. What are the strengths and weaknesses of this idea?

4   Since 2005, bars and pubs in England and Wales with a licence to do so can remain open 24 hours a day. What are the advantages and disadvantages of this idea? Are you in favour of such a change?

# Illegal drugs

This unit looks at the scale and effect of illegal drug-taking in Britain and asks what changes, if any, should be made to deal with this situation.

## A lesson in life

In the summer of 2001, Prince Harry, then aged 16 and third in line to the throne, was discovered by his family to have been involved in under-age drinking and smoking cannabis with a number of his friends in pubs and at parties.

It was reported that shortly after learning of this, his father, Prince Charles, decided to take his son on a visit to a drugs rehabilitation centre in London – presumably with the idea of showing Prince Harry the damage that illegal drugs can cause to people's lives.

▲ The drugs rehabilitation centre that Prince Harry visited with Prince Charles.

## ? Questions

**1** Prince Charles was praised for the way that he handled the situation. What choices did he have? How do you think parents should react in these circumstances?

## Drugs in Britain

There was a great deal of interest about the story in the media, but – perhaps surprisingly – Prince Harry was not heavily criticised. Prince Harry had done something that a lot of young people and adults have done – that is, break the UK drug laws.

**2** Look at the statistics on page 11, and decide whether each statement is correct.

- Young people use illegal drugs more than older people.

- Most people who use drugs do so infrequently.

- Illegal drug-taking appears to have risen between 1998 and 2006.

**3** Why is it difficult to obtain accurate figures of illegal drug-taking in Britain?

**4** Here are three ways in which figures on drug-taking might be obtained. What are the advantages and disadvantages of each? Which method do you think would provide the most accurate picture?

**a** Collect details of all the cases of

# How much goes on?

It is very difficult to be precise about the amount of illegal drug-taking in Britain. The statistics below were the most recent that were available at the time this book was written. They are based on surveys carried out in England and Wales in 2005 and 2006.

## Have you ever used an illegal drug?

|  | Adults aged 16–59 | | Young adults aged 16–24 | |
|---|---|---|---|---|
| 2006 | Yes 35% | No 65% | Yes 45% | No 55% |
| 1998 | Yes 34% | No 66% | Yes 54% | No 46% |

## Have you used an illegal drug in the last month?

|  | Adults aged 16–59 | | Young adults aged 16–24 | |
|---|---|---|---|---|
| 2006 | Yes 6% | No 94% | Yes 15% | No 85% |
| 1998 | Yes 7% | No 93% | Yes 21% | No 79% |

(Source: British Crime Survey 2005–6)

people found guilty in court of possessing or supplying illegal drugs.

**b** Allow the police to record drug use by carrying out a drugs test on everyone they arrest.

**c** Carry out a large survey asking people to indicate whether they have ever used illegal drugs. Assure those taking part that their names and other details would remain confidential.

# The law

The main law covering the use of illegal drugs in Britain is the Misuse of Drugs Act 1971. This Act divides drugs into three groups, or classes, which are designed to reflect the different penalties that may be given for **possession** or **supply**.

**Class A:** Cocaine, crack, ecstasy, heroin, LSD, magic mushrooms, speed (if prepared for injection). Maximum penalties: for possession – 7 years' imprisonment plus fine. For supply – life imprisonment plus fine.

**Class B:** Amphetamines (speed), barbiturates. Maximum penalties: for possession – 5 years' imprisonment plus fine. For supply – 14 years' imprisonment plus fine.

**Class C:** Cannabis, tranquillisers. Maximum penalties: for possession – 2 years' imprisonment plus fine. For supply – 5 years' imprisonment plus fine (14 years for cannabis).

# KeyWords

## Possession

Refers to when someone is knowingly in possession of a controlled (i.e. illegal) drug. A person with a drug in their hand or pocket is almost certainly guilty of possession, so too is someone who has drugs in their car or at home.

## Supply

This describes the situation in which a person sells, gives, or just passes a controlled drug to someone else. Intending or planning to supply a person with illegal drugs is also an offence.

# Illegal drugs

## Starting off

Robbie is 19. He was born in a mining village in Nottinghamshire. He began taking drugs eight years ago, when friends gave him some cannabis.

'It was OK at home until the pit closed. After that there was nothing to do. My dad was out of work, and most people just gave up. Kids started getting into all sorts of things. It was usually glue-sniffing and cannabis at first.

'I was only 11 when I started. Smoking pot made me feel grown-up, especially after I found out how to buy it and then sell it to others. It was a way of making money, and getting my own stuff for free.

'I kept everything together until I was about 15. Some of the older lads smoked heroin. One of them gave me a few lines and told me to try it. "You'll feel great," he said. He was right. I did. I knew what it was doing to me, but in the end I just couldn't stop.

'I was doing quite a lot of crime as well. Partly because of the buzz it gave me, and partly because I needed the money for drugs. I had a mate who worked in an off-licence.

Every week or so, he would turn off the security video while I took some bottles and cans to sell. Then I'd give him something to make it worth his while.

'I didn't go home much, but when I was there I was either half asleep or nicking things. I'd take anything I could sell – my Mum's mobile phone, jewellery, CDs – and cash, of course. When they discovered I'd taken my little sister's new computer they threw me out for good.'

A week ago Robbie was desperate for money to buy drugs and took a bag from a woman in the street, threatening her with a knife. He was caught on video camera and, two days later, arrested by the police.

## Drugs and crime

Recent research has found that heroin and crack cocaine users are four or five times more

likely to commit robbery and shoplifting than offenders who do not use these drugs. Some crack cocaine and heroin users commit more than 200 burglaries a year to fund their habit.

Drug misuse costs the country almost £20 billion a year – that is a cost of about £300 for every member of the population.

## In court

At the police station, Robbie was charged with robbery and the use of an offensive weapon. He was held overnight in a police cell and the following morning appeared in court.

As Robbie already had a criminal record for theft, his solicitor advised him to expect to be given a prison sentence for committing the more serious crime of robbery.

The magistrates realised, however, that Robbie had a severe drug problem.

## Next steps

The judge has to decide whether to punish Robbie's offence with a fine, or a prison sentence. Alternatively, she can issue a community order, which will mean Robbie doing unpaid work in the community.

If the judge passes a community order, she can also require Robbie to have treatment for his addiction. If he refuses, the judge may decide that prison is the only alternative.

# ? Questions

1 How does drug-taking seem to have affected Robbie's life?

2 From the information that you have been given, what reasons can you suggest for Robbie's involvement with drugs? Are there any other reasons not mentioned that you think might be important?

3 Robbie pleads guilty to both charges. What kind of punishment do you think he should be given?

4 What would be best for:
   • society as a whole?
   • the person who Robbie robbed from in the street?
   • Robbie himself?

Explain the reasoning behind each of your answers.

5 Government ministers have said that in the future they hope to cut crime by making drug users who commit serious crimes have compulsory treatment for their addiction. Do you think this is a good idea? What would be the consequences of such a policy?

# Illegal drugs

## Legalising drugs

On 9 July 2002, the Home Secretary, Rt Hon David Blunkett MP, spoke to MPs in the House of Commons on the subject of drugs.

'I cannot imagine that there is a member of this House who does not wish to ensure that those we represent are free from the misery that is caused by drug abuse.

'Over the last 30 years the huge increase in the use of drugs, particularly hard drugs, has caused untold damage to the health, life chances, and well-being of individuals. This has undermined family life, fuelled criminality, and damaged communities.

'We will not legalise or decriminalise any drug, nor do we envisage a time when this would be appropriate.'

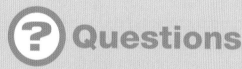 **Questions**

**1** What is Mr Blunkett's view of illegal drugs?

**2** Do you agree with him? Are there any parts of his speech that you disagree with?

## Another way

As drug-taking has damaged and destroyed so many lives, it seems only common sense that the use of drugs should be banned. However, there are a number of people who argue that some of these problems could be avoided if some drugs became legal.

## The case for legalising drugs

Those in favour of legalising drugs argue that using drugs should be allowed through specially licensed dealers, who would be controlled by law and regularly checked. Laws would prohibit drugs being sold to young people below a certain age. Here are some of the arguments that they use.

 **Drug laws are failing**
Crime figures show that the present laws controlling drugs are not working. Making drugs illegal does not stop people from using them.

 **Crime and violence**
When drugs are illegal, buyers and sellers use violence to sort out disagreements. They can't use the courts or any of the other usual methods because the trade that they are involved in is against the law.

 **Police and court time**
Dealing with drug crime takes a huge amount of time and money that could be better spent trying to prevent or solve other crimes.

 **Greater health risks**
At the moment, it is impossible for drug users to know the quality and purity of the drugs they are buying. This can be very dangerous. It would be much less of a problem if drugs were sold through specially licensed dealers.

 **Income**
If drugs were sold legally, a small tax could be imposed that could provide the government with money for healthcare to help people come off drugs.

**3** Look at the points opposite in favour of legalising drugs, and try to think of an argument that could be made against each one.

**4** If the government decides to change its policy towards drugs it has a number of choices. It can:

- leave the law as it is
- legalise all drugs and make them available only through licensed dealers
- legalise *some* drugs, and leave the rest illegal
- *increase* punishments for those found using or selling illegal drugs.

What would you suggest it should do, and why?

# Two sides to the problem

### In favour

Although his son, Scott, died of a heroin overdose, Mr Gillespie believes that drugs should be legalised. 'I wish people wouldn't use them,' he says, 'but they do, and we need to put some order into the market.'

Scott Gillespie took drugs for many years, but was forced to do without them when he was sent to prison for five weeks. As soon as he was released, he went in search of a fix, but the dose that he gave himself was too large – and impure. Mr Gillespie believes that his son would still be alive if the heroin had been supplied legally and in a controlled environment.

AMPHETAMINES  ECSTASY

HEROIN

CANNABIS

COCAINE

LSD

### Against

'I have a 14-year-old son, who is at an age when he is tempted to try new and interesting things. I trust his sense of right and wrong, but know that young people come under strong peer pressure. When drugs are against the law, my son can say, "No I'm not trying that because it is against the law."

If that reason is removed and drugs are legalised, where does that leave him? If society tells my son that drugs are OK, then I hate to think where that may lead – keep drugs illegal.'

(Source: From an email on the BBC discussion board.)

# The big issue

Obesity – that is, being seriously overweight – is now a major problem in many countries. In this unit, we ask who is responsible for this and what should be done to improve our nation's health.

## Eating can damage your health

In 2002, a group of American teenagers and their parents served a lawsuit against fast food manufacturer McDonald's, claiming that the company was responsible for making the young people fat.

They argued that McDonald's had broken New York state law by deliberately misleading customers into thinking that their products were healthy and nutritious. They said that the company did not provide information on the health risks of eating fast food, and claimed that the young people had developed health problems such as obesity, diabetes and high blood pressure through eating the company's products.

One parent stated that she wouldn't have let her son eat so many Big Macs and fries if she had realised the damage that they would cause. Her son, aged 15, weighed over 180 kilograms (about 28 stone).

## Pressure

The lawyer representing the young people and their families claimed that children who regularly ate fast food meals more than once a week ran the risk of developing health problems. 'Nobody thinks about this,' he said, 'because the food is promoted as being healthy.'

The lawyer argued that, with so many advertisements and promotions, it was difficult for parents and children to resist McDonald's offers of toys with their meals.

## Defence

In reply, McDonald's said that people have known for a long time about the damage caused by eating too many hamburgers and fries. People should know what harm they are doing to themselves if they have a poor diet and do not take enough exercise.

## Warning signs

Most people know that beefburgers, chips and ice cream are fattening – but what do we know about the contents of other foods that we buy?

## Salt

Snack foods like crisps, pasta shapes, and baked beans usually contain large amounts of salt. Salt is an important part of our diet, but too much causes serious health problems, like strokes and heart disease. A leading heart specialist recently stated that a cut of ten per cent of the salt in the average diet would save the lives of 5,800 people in a year.

## Sugar

Many manufactured food products also contain large amounts of sugar. A medium-sized (500ml) bottle of cola is likely to contain the equivalent of ten spoonfuls of sugar.

Too much sugar in a diet brings problems of tooth decay and weight gain. It can also lead to diabetes – a life-threatening condition, in which a person has too much sugar in their blood. For the first time ever, this particular type of diabetes is now being found amongst teenagers in Britain.

## ? Questions

1   What arguments can you suggest in support of the claim against McDonald's by the teenagers and their parents? What arguments can you suggest against it?

2   Sometimes people say that making healthy eating choices is harder than making unhealthy ones. Do you agree with this statement? Explain your thinking.

3   The New York judge decided that McDonald's was not to blame for the young people's weight problems and that the company could not be held responsible if customers chose to eat too many of its products. Do you agree with this decision?

4   Look at some of the items in your fridge or store cupboard at home. Think about:

   • What kind of information is given on the side of tins or packets of food
   • how helpful the information is
   • what the information does or doesn't tell you.

   Would any further information be useful?

5   Snack food manufacturers have been criticised for targeting children and young people in the advertising and marketing of their products. Can you think of any evidence that supports this view? Why do you think they have been criticised for this?

6   How much responsibility do food manufacturers have to produce food that is not damaging to health?

# The big issue

## Size counts

After trying for more than six years to have a baby, Yvonne and her husband decided to apply to an adoption agency. During the first interview Yvonne was advised her application could be affected by her weight. Yvonne describes herself as 5'4" and a plump 12 stone. 'It's not ideal,' she said, 'but I didn't realise it could prevent us from adopting a child.'

The social worker explained that parents who wanted to adopt had to undergo a medical – and a person who is overweight may be refused.

Difficulties can be experienced by overweight people in other areas of life. There are cases of overweight people being refused or dismissed from work or having medical treatment withheld until they lose a certain amount of weight.

### A growing concern

Over the last hundred years, the average weight of people in Britain has been steadily rising. For most of this time, this has not been a problem. In the past, many people's weight has been below the recommended level.

In the last ten years, however, there have been signs that a large number of people are becoming overweight.

- About 40 per cent of adults in Britain are overweight.
- A further 20 per cent are obese.
- In the last ten years, obesity rates have risen by nearly 50 per cent.

## Overweight or obese?

The main measure of obesity is known as the Body Mass Index (BMI). To calculate your BMI, divide your weight in kilograms by your height in metres, squared. A figure below 18.5 is regarded as underweight, between 25–29.9 overweight, and 30 or above, obese.

Someone who is 1.75m tall and weighs 90 kilos has a BMI of $90 \div 1.75^2 = 29.41$, making them seriously overweight.

### Putting on weight

Obesity is a problem in many countries throughout the world. Obesity levels have risen because people take less exercise and obtain their food in different ways from how they did in the past.

**? Questions ? ? ?**

1  What are the consequences of a person being overweight or obese?

▲ A factory food production line.

## Factory food

Until the 1970s most of the food that we ate was prepared and cooked at home. Today, much more food is made in factories.

Factory production reduces the time needed to prepare food. Cakes, biscuits, puddings, and whole meals that take a lot of time to prepare in the home, can now be mass-produced in a factory at relatively low cost.

This gives people a much wider choice over what to eat, and makes high-calorific (i.e. fattening) food much more easily available.

## Exercise

Home entertainment – such as television and computers – and widespread car ownership mean that we exercise a great deal less than we used to. A half-hour walk each day would reduce cases of obesity by one-third.

2  Is it fair to discriminate in employment against people who are overweight? Try to give reasons for your answer.

3  Here are some suggestions for reducing the number of young people who are overweight. Select two or three and suggest the benefits and drawbacks of each one.

**Tax**  Place an extra tax on foods with a high fat, salt or sugar content.

**Warnings**  Put health warnings on food products with high levels of fat, salt or sugar.

**Fitness**  Have more sport and PE lessons in school.

**Inspections**  Inspect schools for the fitness of their students as well as their academic performance.

**Ban**  Remove all food and drink vending machines from schools (as they have done in France).

**Money**  Offer a financial reward for people to lose weight (this has been tried in Italy).

4  Who is responsible for what we eat? What part should the government play in controlling people's diet and exercise?

# The information age

This unit explains the meaning of the term 'mass media' and asks what purpose our newspapers should serve.

## Monday morning

Sam woke up to the sound of the radio alarm. 'You're listening to Radio One, it's 7.23, and here's Britney…'. She leaned over and switched off – not her favourite singer. She heard noises from downstairs. Her brother and sister were already up and watching cartoons on the television.

It was all coming back. Yesterday afternoon Sam had gone to the cinema with a friend. She didn't do much in the evening, except look at a magazine and read her book. The geography homework just slipped her mind. It was her turn to make a presentation to the class. She jumped out of bed and turned on her computer. Maybe she could find the answers there – she just needed a short article on climate change and she'd be fine.

Downstairs young Tommy and Belinda were sitting on the sofa spooning cereal into their mouths, glued to the cartoons. Their father walked into the room and switched the channel to the news.

'We were watching that,' said Tommy.

'Go and clean your teeth and make sure you're ready to go,' Dad replied. 'I need to see the traffic report and hear the headlines before I take you to the station.'

Eventually, Sam, Tommy and Belinda were all loaded into the car with bags and lunches. Their father ran back into the house for the newspaper to read during his lunch-break; and then they were off. As they turned onto the main road, Sam noticed a new hoarding. A woman with gleaming white teeth stared down at passers-by. 'Buy this toothpaste,' she seemed to be saying, 'and you too can be young and beautiful.'

'Blast,' thought Sam, 'I forgot to clean my teeth.'

## 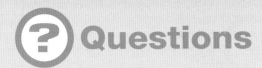 Questions

**1** What are the different forms of **mass media** mentioned in this story?

**2** How was each of these forms of mass media used by the members of Sam's family?

**3** Which media do you use most for:
- learning about the news?
- entertainment?
- relaxation?

Explain your reasons for each choice.

**4** News is now available to many people 24 hours a day, seven days a week. What are the advantages of this?

Are there any disadvantages? If so, explain what you think they are.

**5** Today, more than 60 per cent of households in Britain are online, compared with nine per cent in 1998. What are the benefits of the Internet? What are the problems?

**6** Make a note of the advertisements immediately before, during and after a popular children's television programme. Which group of people is each advertisement aimed at?

**7** Today, companies often advertise in schools, putting their names on books, vending machines and teaching resources. What are the benefits and disadvantages of this?

---

## NEWSXTRA

### Advertising

Almost all the mass media today carry advertisements. That is how the various media are usually paid for. Companies spend billions of pounds advertising their products, and use all kinds of ways to get their message across.

Sometimes the message comes directly through advertisements. On other occasions it's more subtle. Large companies sponsor sports events and popular TV programmes. Sometimes companies pay for their products to be used on a film or television programme. This is banned in Britain, but is common in the United States.

By 2009, junk food adverts will be banned on all children's TV channels, but some people feel the ban should go further. They would like a ban on all adverts for junk food shown before 9p.m.

### Online

Scientists in California have estimated that we have produced and stored more information in the last five years than for the rest of history put together.

### 24/7

Many people today, if they choose, can watch or listen to programmes at all times of the day or night. Television, radio and the Internet bring news to people quicker than at any time in history. In September 2001, millions of people throughout the world watched events unfold on television during the terrorist attack on the World Trade Center in New York.

### KeyWords

**Mass media**

Means of communication that reach large numbers of people – such as books, newspapers, radio, television and the Internet.

# Daily news

## The front page

The evening before a newspaper is published, the editor and senior journalists meet to decide which story should go on the front page. The story they choose will be the first thing that anyone thinking of buying the paper will see. Choosing the right story therefore affects sales of the paper.

Here are some of the news stories on one day in 2007.

The sacking of the chief police officer investigating the disappearance of Madeleine McCann.

RECORD HIGH TEMPERATURES IN THE ARCTIC.

The man who is trying to avoid paying a £2m gambling debt.

The Prime Minister's decision to reduce the numbers of British troops in Iraq.

Pictures, not previously released, of the moments just before the car crash in Paris in which Princess Diana was killed.

The Conservative Party's plans to cut taxes if they win the next election.

Footballer Steven Gerrard meets a ten-year-old boy with whom he was involved in a car accident.

Unconfirmed news that a general election will take place in less than a month.

FEWER CHILDREN HAVE SCHOOL DINNERS.

## Daily UK newspaper sales

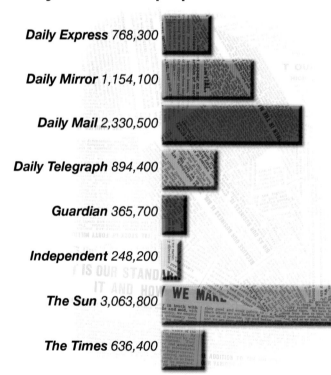

Daily Express 768,300

Daily Mirror 1,154,100

Daily Mail 2,330,500

Daily Telegraph 894,400

Guardian 365,700

Independent 248,200

The Sun 3,063,800

The Times 636,400

(Source: Audit Bureau of Circulations 2007)

## Stumped

When Katherine walked into her local newsagent's she was surprised to see herself on the front page of the *Sunday Mirror*. She had just come back from Barbados where she had been playing at a music festival.

Katherine was pictured, wearing a revealing low-cut dress, with David Gower – former England cricket captain, sports quiz panellist and commentator – standing behind her, with his arms around her.

Alongside the picture ran the headline: 'Howzat! What WAS cricket hero David Gower up to in a Caribbean bar at 2 in the morning?'

In fact, the answer was: nothing. At the end of the festival, Katherine and some of the other musicians had gone to a bar for a few drinks, where they met David Gower and other cricket commentators. They all talked for a while, and then David Gower showed Katherine, and some of the others in her group, how to hold a cricket bat. This was when the front page photograph was taken. David Gower left the bar around 3a.m. and Katherine left about an hour later.

There was no relationship between Katherine and David Gower, despite the story beginning with the claim that the former England captain had 'made a tipsy bid to bowl a maiden over'.

# Freedom of the press

## Uncovering the truth

In 1972, preparations were taking place in America for the US presidential election. There were two candidates, President Richard Nixon, standing for the Republican Party, and George McGovern, candidate for the Democrats.

During the early hours of the morning of 17 June 1972, police discovered five men inside Watergate – the large hotel and office building in Washington DC that the Democrats were using as their campaign headquarters. The burglars were there to photograph secret documents belonging to the Democrats and to adjust bugging equipment that they had secretly installed a month before.

Newspapers claimed that one of the burglars worked for the Republican Party – the Democrats' opposition – but the Republicans denied involvement in the break-in. However, some journalists started to look at the case more closely. Six weeks later they reported that one of the burglars had paid a cheque for $25,000 into his bank account. The money had come from the Republicans.

In November 1972, Richard Nixon easily won the presidential election, but journalists and investigators continued to try to find out whether the bugging had been done with the President's approval. Eventually, enough evidence was gathered to show that it had, and that Mr Nixon had repeatedly lied when he denied any involvement. Richard Nixon was charged with 'high crimes and misdemeanours' and resigned as president just before he was due to face trial.

▲ Richard Nixon, on the right, just after he resigned the presidency of the USA in 1974.

## Freedom of speech

Vietnamese journalist Nguyen Vu Binh wrote several newspaper articles criticising his government. In July 2002, he was questioned by police over 'activities harming public order and public security'. Material was taken from his computer.

Later that year he was arrested again, this time for criticising agreements his country had made over border arrangements with China.

In 2003, Nguyen Vu Binh was charged and found guilty of espionage in a trial that lasted three hours. For this he was sentenced to seven years in prison. Although Vietnam's law guarantees a **free press**, newspapers run the risk of being closed down if they criticise the government harshly.

1 What are the main differences between these stories?

2 Should newspapers be allowed to publish stories that are critical of their government?

3 What are the advantages in allowing this? What are the disadvantages?

## The public interest, or interesting to the public?

All newspapers print news about the lives of celebrities. This sometimes involves stories about love affairs, marriage break-ups, or serious illnesses. Newspapers often sell more copies with stories of this kind. However, some people complain that these articles are hurtful and unnecessary, and accuse the press of invading people's **privacy**.

4 Which of the stories below are interesting to you? Which do you think are in the **public interest**? Explain your answer.

- The teenage daughter of a well-known soap star actress has been taking drugs at parties.
- A famous actress has a drug addiction problem that she is trying to keep secret.
- A politician has an affair with another woman, whilst his wife is expecting a baby.
- A newborn baby dies. Two years before, the baby's father lost another child, with a different partner, at the same maternity unit.

5 In what circumstances might it be worth publishing those stories that you thought were *not* in the public interest?

## KeyWords

### Free press
Freedom for the media to write or express an opinion and give information.

### Privacy
Freedom from public attention or intrusion in personal affairs.

### Public interest
Action taken to benefit the public as a whole.

# Finding the truth

## Saving Private Lynch

During the second Iraq war, in March 2003, a small convoy group of American army vehicles was ambushed by Iraqi forces. Nine Americans were killed, and several reported missing. One of those was 19-year-old Private Jessica Lynch who, it was later discovered, had been injured and taken to hospital by Iraqi special police.

Ten days after the attack, senior US officials announced that American forces had stormed the hospital where Private Lynch was being held in a daring assault to rescue the injured soldier. Much of this was recorded on night-vision cameras, showing heavily armed forces entering the hospital and then carrying Private Lynch to a waiting helicopter. The injured soldier was lying on a stretcher, wrapped in a blanket, with the stars and stripes flag draped over her shoulder.

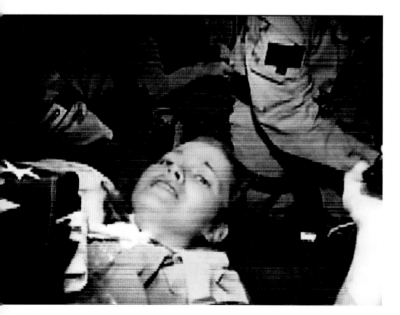

US General Brooks told the press, 'Some brave souls put their lives on the line to make this happen'.

Shortly after the rescue, journalists were told that Private Lynch received stab and bullet wounds as she tried to resist capture and had been interrogated and assaulted during her time in hospital.

### ? Questions

1 If you were an American reading this story, how would you have felt about:
  • Jessica Lynch?
  • US Special Forces in Iraq?
  • the Iraqis?

## A hero's return

Jessica Lynch returned to America a hero. But during the months that followed it began to appear that some of the facts were not as they first seemed.

Private Lynch had not been involved in a shoot-out with Iraqi forces. In fact, she hadn't used her rifle at all. Iraqi doctors found no evidence of shot or stab wounds and Jessica herself has no memory of these either. Her injuries, it seems, were caused by the rocket-propelled grenade that hit her vehicle.

She had been brought to hospital unconscious and in shock from blood loss, where Iraqi doctors worked as best they could to save her life.

When American forces arrived at the hospital there was no resistance. The Iraqi soldiers had left the day before, something that was probably already known to the Americans. Many now believe that the rescue was stage-managed – welcome publicity in a difficult war.

2   Why do you think Jessica's actions and those of US forces were initially presented in the way that they were?

3   What does this tell you about the way news stories can be managed?

4   Is there a case for creating 'good news' stories that aren't wholly true when your country is fighting a war?

5   Look at the two versions of the same fictional story (right). How has it been presented differently?

6   What is the best way of finding out what's going on? Is there any part of the media that is more accurate than others?

# Spinning the news

**Anyone who tells a story or describes a series of events sets out the information in the way that they would like the events to be understood.**

**When governments, businesses or other organisations do this, it is known as 'spinning the news' – picking out the particular pieces of news they want the media to feature in their stories, and leaving out those that they do not.**

**The people who do it are called 'spin doctors'. They try to stop any negative statements about a person or their organisation coming out so that they appear in the best possible light.**

## 500 sacked in shock move by computer company

Computer manufacturer Chip announced yesterday that 500 workers are to lose their jobs at their two Scottish factories. Workers were given no warning and have little hope of finding new work in areas where unemployment is already high. Jean Finch, who works on the production line, said, 'I am devastated. No one told us this might happen. My husband is not working and we may lose our house if I can't pay the mortgage.'

### Thousands of jobs saved by Chip's chop

After the recent fall in profits, the computer company, Chip, took swift action today to cut costs by closing two of its plants. The company said this would protect the jobs of the 1,500 workers who will remain with the company, and that it would provide a re-training package for the workers who had been made redundant. John Hanson, finance director, said: 'This will create a leaner, more competitive company, which will mean better opportunities for our workforce in the future.'

# Transport matters

In this unit we look at some of the reasons for increased traffic levels, the damage this causes and methods being used to reduce the number of cars in our towns and cities.

## You'll be late!

Every morning, Robert's mum shouts at him to hurry up and come downstairs for breakfast. He grabs a quick bowl of cereal, picks up his PE kit, packed lunch and school bag, and rushes out of the house. He jumps into his mother's car, which has the engine already running, to travel the journey of about a mile to school.

When they arrive, his mother gets cross because once again she can't find anywhere in the road outside the school to park. She tells him to jump out while she pulls in a bit – and to look out for other cars.

Robert races into school as the bell is ringing. He calls out 'Hi' to his friend Muhammad, who lives in his road but is in another class. He thinks it would be nice to stroll to school with Muhammad and talk about his new computer game, but Muhammad's dad drops him off earlier on his way to work and Robert will have to wait until break to see him.

Meanwhile, his mum is having trouble getting out of the road – there are so many other cars all manoeuvring out of the side road into the busy High Street. Still, she feels relieved to see Robert into school. She worries about him. He is only nine and she thinks some harm might come to him if she didn't take him to school herself.

## ? Questions

1 Why do so many parents drive their children to school?

2 What are the advantages and disadvantages of this?

## The school run

- 20 years ago about one in three children in primary schools made their own way to school. Today it is about one in nine.
- The number of journeys to school by car has nearly doubled in the last ten years.
- Around 8.50a.m. in term time, one in every five cars on roads in towns and cities is taking children to school.
- School runs make the journeys of other car drivers up to 50 per cent longer in some parts of the country.

## The problem

Many parents worry that their children might be harmed by traffic or by child abductors. They feel more relaxed when they know that their children have arrived safely. However, some children say that they would prefer to walk to school with friends, to have some time to chat about their interests and hobbies. Walking or cycling would be better for their health too. Lack of exercise is one reason why children today are more likely to be overweight than they used to be.

Lots of traffic also brings problems of air pollution. Children can be affected by air pollution even if they are inside a car.

## Some solutions

### Walking buses

A 'walking bus' lets a group, or 'bus', of children walk from home to school each morning quickly and safely under the guidance of trained adult supervisors.

### No stopping

Parents in one London borough may drive their children to school only if they have a special permit to stop outside the school.

3 Here are some more ways of discouraging the school run.

- Create car 'exclusion zones' around schools to force parents and children to walk to school.

- Employ more 'lollipop' men and women.

- Add more special cycle paths.

- Make sure that all schools have proper bike sheds, where bicycles can be safely left.

- Ban the use of large 4x4 vehicles on the school run.

- Provide special free bus services to take children to school, like the yellow school buses used in the US.

a Say what you think of each one.

b Are there any other suggestions you would add?

4 Only a limited number of stopping permits (see left) are available. How do you think schools should decide which parents should receive a permit?

# Transport matters

## Rush hour

### Stuck in traffic!

All towns and cities in Britain suffer from **traffic congestion** at some time during the day. Most were built long before the car was invented and there is not enough room for all the vehicles on the roads. Many people now own a car, and one in four households owns two cars.

Around 85 per cent of journeys are made by cars, vans and taxis. Only 12 per cent are made on public transport.

Over the last 20 years, road traffic has grown by 20 per cent, and is increasing by about three per cent each year.

### Shopping

Today, we travel further to buy food and other goods for the home, and the transportation of food accounts for about half the lorry journeys in Britain.

### Cost

Over the last 15–20 years, the relative cost of motoring has remained just about the same. The cost of bus fares has risen by over 30 per cent, and some train fares by much more than this.

## THE EFFECTS OF CONGESTION

### Air pollution

Cars push out pollutants into the air, particularly carbon dioxide ($CO_2$). These are not only bad for our health and affect our breathing (causing asthma attacks), they are also greenhouse gases, which contribute to global warming. Most of these gases are produced when cars are travelling slowly, so traffic jams are very bad for air quality. It is believed that traffic fumes contribute to thousands of deaths each year.

### Noise

Traffic also creates a lot of noise that has a bad effect on people living and working on or near busy roads, causing stress and reducing their quality of life.

### Delays

A quarter of Britain's main roads are jammed for an hour a day. Delays cause frustration for drivers and people using buses.

### Costs to the economy

Traffic jams mean that businesses are losing money because workers lose time, and delivery vehicles take longer to make journeys, as well as using more fuel. The cost to businesses is estimated to be £20 billion a year.

# ❓ Questions

**1** Is it possible to do nothing about traffic problems?

**2** Look at the ideas below and decide which ones you agree with. Choose three solutions and prepare a case to argue for each one.

- Build more roads.
- Stop people bringing their cars into cities by increasing parking charges.
- Make more bus lanes.
- Reduce train, bus and tram fares.
- Encourage car-sharing by providing special lanes for cars carrying two people or more. This is common in the US.

- Create more cycle lanes.
- Cut down travel by encouraging firms to let employees work at home, where possible.
- Slow vehicles down with road humps and zigzag routes.

- Make motorists pay for the distance that they drive.

PAY HERE

- **Pedestrianisation**: remove cars from city centres.

**3** Almost all of these ideas would require new rules and laws. Select one of the solutions that you originally chose, and try to draft the wording of the rule or law that would put the measure into practice.

# KeyWords

## Pedestrianisation
Closing central areas in towns and cities to cars.

## Traffic congestion
Very slow moving traffic, caused by too many vehicles in an area.

31

# Transport matters

## Congestion charging

### Steer clear of the city

In 2003, the then Mayor of London, Ken Livingstone, introduced a plan to reduce traffic congestion in London – the **congestion charge**.

Anyone driving a vehicle into central London between 7a.m. and 6p.m. (Monday to Friday) has to pay £8 a day. Some drivers, for example those with disabilities, do not have to pay. People living inside the charging zone receive a 90 per cent discount. There is no charge for public buses, taxis, motorcycles, bicycles or electric vehicles, but the vast majority of people travelling by car have to pay.

### A good move

The scheme has been hailed as a great success. Statistics produced by the organisation that is responsible for London's transport system show that:

- traffic in central London has been cut by 20 per cent with 70,000 fewer cars entering the zone, each day
- more people now travel on buses than at any time since 1965
- carbon dioxide emissions from traffic are down by 16 per cent
- the charge earns about £90 million for the City.

Mr Livingstone has said: 'Congestion charging was a radical solution to a long-standing problem. London's roads were clogged with slow-moving traffic and congestion was costing business £2 million a week. Despite the dire predictions before the launch of the scheme, congestion charging has proved a success, and that is why 75 per cent of Londoners now support the scheme.'

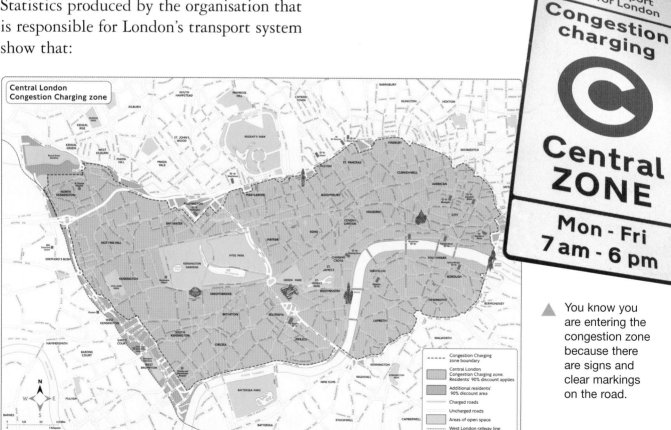

You know you are entering the congestion zone because there are signs and clear markings on the road.

## Opposition

Not everybody is in favour of the charge. Some shopkeepers claim that customer numbers have fallen. Others say that public transport should have been improved first because it is not reliable enough or adequate to carry the numbers of people who use it every day.

Some lower paid workers who have to drive into the centre feel that the charge hits them unfairly. Opponents also say that traffic congestion is starting to creep up again and is close to the level it was when the charge was introduced.

## Taking it further

Other cities are seriously considering some sort of charge. In 2007, councils in Manchester voted to bring in a congestion charge to a large area of the city, making it the biggest scheme of its kind in the world. Cardiff is also looking at the idea of using a congestion charge to pay for improvements in transport.

It is not only in the UK that there has been interest in the London experiment. Cities like Stockholm, Barcelona and Milan are thinking about having similar schemes.

Some people think that some sort of **road pricing** is the only way to control exploding traffic growth and reduce fast-growing car use. It's not just about slow traffic; it's about the health of the people who live in cities.

## ? Questions

1   Look at the information in the text on the previous page. Do you think that the congestion charge has been a success or a failure? Explain why.

2   Draw up a list of those people who benefit from the congestion charge in London, and those who do not.

3   Another idea being considered by the government is to require all vehicles to be fitted with a small transmitter so that they could be tracked by satellite, wherever they go. The system would charge users based on the miles they travelled. A higher charge would be made for travel during periods of congestion.

What are the strengths and weaknesses of this idea? Would it make our country a better place to live in? Would you be prepared to support this idea?

## Key**Words**

### Congestion charge
A charge or fee paid to enter an area where traffic is very heavy.

### Road pricing
Paying for using the roads.

# What is politics?

This unit looks at the meaning of politics and what makes something political.

## Racists and bullies

Maia is 14 years old. One morning, on the way to school, she noticed three boys in her year group picking on two boys in Year 7, both from an Asian background. She saw the same thing the next day. A week later, she found herself standing behind the same two Year 7 students in the dinner queue, when the three older boys pushed in.

'Didn't think either of you would be eating here,' one of the older boys said to the younger pupils. 'Not your sort of thing, is it?'

'Maybe they've got curry on the menu,' said his friend, laughing.

Maia started to feel very angry. She hated all forms of racism. How dare they say things like that.

## ? Questions

1 Maia felt she ought to do something. What are her choices? Make a list of the different things she could do in this situation. Which would be the best and worst? Explain why.

## Taking action

Maia decided to cause a fuss. She told the three boys that they had no right to speak like that. 'It's racist,' she said, adding, 'and you're not pushing in ahead of me.'

Later in the day, Maia told one of her friends about what had happened. 'I feel quite pleased,' she said. 'That's my good turn for the day.'

'And what's going to happen tomorrow?' said Dionne. 'They'll do the same thing to some other poor kid.

'You're good at speaking out,' Dionne told Maia. 'You've got to do something more. There's a lot of bullying in this school and people get away with all kinds of racist behaviour. It makes some kids' lives absolute hell.'

2 Read through each of Maia's ideas on the next page. Are there any that you would add? Are there any that you think she should reject?

3 Which ideas do you think would be the most effective in dealing with the problem of bullying and racism at school?

# Going further

**Maia thinks about what she can do.**

**• Teachers**
Report the three bullies to her form tutor, or any other teacher she knows well.

**• School council**
Raise the matter with the school council.

**• Head teacher**
Arrange a meeting with the head teacher or other senior staff. Ask them what action they intend to take to reduce bullying and racist behaviour at school.

STOP RACISM & BULLYING

REPORT RACIST INCIDENTS
OR BULLYING
TO YOUR HEAD OF YEAR

**• Posters**
Put up some posters round the school, telling people to report racist incidents or bullying to their Head of Year.

**• Media**
Write a letter to the local newspaper criticising the school for not doing enough about bullying and racism.

**• Petition**
Get signatures from as many students and parents as possible demanding stronger action by the school on bullying and racism.

LETTERS ✉

**School policy on bullying and racism is useless**

STOP RACISM & BULLYING

## Getting political

Maia spoke at the next school council meeting, asking teachers to take racist incidents at the school much more seriously. Dionne organised a petition, which she and Maia gave to Mrs Bentley, their Head of Year. Mrs Bentley agreed to set up a meeting in which students could tell staff about the kinds of racist behaviour that took place in school. About 40 students attended.

Over the next year Maia and Dionne found themselves meeting people from the local council, organising an anti-racism conference in school, and working with teachers to find ways of reducing bullying.

## Politics

Maia and Dionne got involved in politics the moment they decided to try to do something about the problems of bullying and racism in their school. Politics is the business of deciding what sort of society we want and how to deal with problems that affect society.

4 Think of at least three political issues that society is facing today. (One could be local, one national and the other international.)

5 Now take one of these problems and explain why it is a political issue and suggest at least one way in which it could be solved.

# Reaching a decision

This unit looks at the ways in which important government decisions can be made.

## All change

Britain is one of only a few countries where vehicles are driven on the left-hand side of the road.

Imagine that this rule is to be changed, so that Britain can join France, Germany, Spain and most other European countries by driving on the right.

### Government in Britain

If this decision had to be taken in Britain, it would probably be made by Members of Parliament (MPs) after discussion with experts, motoring organisations and many of the other groups of people who would be affected by the change.

## ? Questions

**1** How should a decision like this be taken? Here are some different ways in which it could be done. What are the strengths and weaknesses of each one?

**Experts** Allow the police and road safety experts to decide.

**Government** Let the Prime Minister and other senior members of the government decide on behalf of the country.

**Members of Parliament (MPs)** Let the final decision be made by MPs who would debate the matter in the House of Commons, and then vote on whether the change should be made.

**Monarchy** Allow the Queen (or King) to make the decision.

**Motorists and drivers** Hold a vote amongst everyone with a driving licence.

**Referendum** Give all voters (whether drivers or not) the opportunity to vote on whether to make the change.

**2** What, in your view, would be the best way to make a decision of this kind? Would it be the fairest? Explain your answer.

# Members of Parliament

There are 646 Members of Parliament. MPs almost always belong to a political party and always represent a particular area of the country (known as a 'constituency'). MPs must be aged 18 or over, and must stand for election at least every five years.

## The working week

Most MPs spend at least six days a week at work, splitting their time between their constituency and the House of Commons in London.

## In their constituency

MPs support the area in whatever way they can. This might mean talking to local business people, visiting schools and community groups, meeting people who live in their constituency, or helping in some way with local problems.

Most MPs hold a 'surgery' on Friday or Saturday, where local residents can ask for advice or help, or draw a particular problem to their attention.

## In the House of Commons

MPs spend a great deal of time in meeting and committee rooms advising and checking on the government's work. Most MPs do not go into the Chamber every day where we see debates take place. Some take part in formal debates only occasionally. All MPs have subjects that interest them, on which they speak for their party – for example: Northern Ireland, the environment or transport.

If an MP is not in a meeting or taking part in a debate in the House of Commons, they are probably dealing with requests for help from constituents or, in the evening, talking to other MPs or political contacts.

MPs speaking in the House of Commons ▶
debating chamber. This image is taken
from a televised debate.

3  What do you think makes a good MP? Explain your thinking.

4  MPs have opinions on most of the big issues of the day, and they usually agree with their party's policy. But what should they do if they do not? What is more important – the constituents, the party or an MP's conscience?

a  Parliament is due to vote on a new law requiring everyone to have an identity card. Some MPs are in favour of this – but know that their constituents are not. How should they vote?

b  A vote is to be held in Parliament on whether a referendum should be held on the new European constitution. A group of Labour MPs are in favour of this, but their party is against it. If the Labour MPs vote for a referendum, the government is likely to be defeated, and their own party will be damaged. What should they do?

# Voting

This unit explains who can and cannot vote at elections in Britain, and asks if any of these rules should be changed.

## Equal rights

The right to vote is something that most people in Britain take for granted. But this has not always been the case. Two hundred years ago, only two per cent of the population could vote, and all were wealthy *men*. Most men in Britain gained the right to vote during the nineteenth century. It wasn't until 1928 that women and men had the same voting rights (see page 40).

## ? Questions

1 Using the information below, decide which of the following people would be able to vote at a **general election** in Britain:

**Henri**, aged 22, a French citizen, living in Paris, is staying in Wales on holiday for two weeks.

**Joanne**, aged 30, was born and lived in Ireland. Last year she started working as a nurse at a hospital in Nottingham, where her name is on the electoral roll.

## Who can vote?

Today, voters must be:
- aged 18 or over
- citizens of the United Kingdom, the Commonwealth or a European Union member state, and
- have their name on the **electoral register**.

Citizens of the UK, the Commonwealth and Ireland living in this country may vote in all public elections.

Citizens of European Union states (see page 46), living in the UK, can vote in local and European elections, but not in elections to the Parliament in London.

## Who can't vote?

Those who cannot vote at elections include:
- anyone under 18 years of age
- members of the House of Lords
- Church of England bishops and archbishops
- prisoners serving a sentence for a criminal conviction
- those with learning disabilities or a mental illness that the authorities believe prevents them from making a reasoned judgement on the day of the election.

**Margaret**, aged 94, is almost blind, and lives in a home for the elderly. Her name is on the local electoral roll.

**Perry**, aged 23, from Sheffield, now serving a six-month prison sentence for selling cannabis.

**Stacey**, aged 17, was born and lives in south-east London, where she is now studying for her A levels at college.

## At what age?

In 1969, the voting age in Britain was lowered from 21 to 18. It is now being suggested that it should be further reduced to 16. Here are some views about this.

**a** If 16 and 17 year olds can gamble, work, join the army and get married, why shouldn't they be able to vote?

**b** Most adults and many teenagers are not in favour of reducing the voting age to 16.

**c** Teenagers don't have the maturity or understanding to use the vote sensibly.

**d** 16 and 17 year olds have a lot to say about what's going on and should be listened to.

**e** Young people aren't interested in politics and voting.

**f** The number of young people who demonstrated against the war in Iraq in 2003 shows that young people are interested in politics.

## Throughout the world

The voting age in most countries is 18 years of age. However, in Japan it is 20, in Malaysia 21 – and in Austria and the Isle of Man, it is 16 years of age.

**2** Sort out statements a–f (below left) into those in favour of, and those against lowering the voting age to 16.

**3** Should the voting age be changed? Explain your view.

**4** If the voting age was lowered to 16, there would be at least one and a half million more people eligible to vote. What might be the effect of this large number of young voters on government policies?

## Key**Words**

### Electoral register
A list of all those people in a particular area who are entitled to vote.

### General election
The day on which all 646 Members of Parliament (MPs) stand for election to the House of Commons in London. General elections must be held at least every five years, but may be called more often.

# Voting

## Going to the polls

### Elections

General and **European elections** are held at least every four or five years in Britain. People living in Northern Ireland, Wales and Scotland also vote for members of their own national assemblies or parliaments.

Voter turnout for the 2001 general election was the lowest of any election since 1918. For the next election, in 2005, the figure rose by two per cent.

### Voter turnout

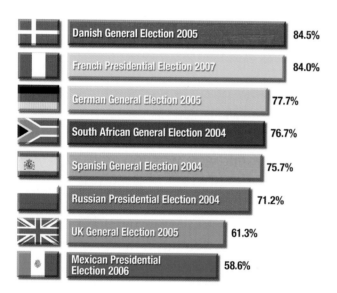

| | Election | Turnout |
|---|---|---|
| | Danish General Election 2005 | 84.5% |
| | French Presidential Election 2007 | 84.0% |
| | German General Election 2005 | 77.7% |
| | South African General Election 2004 | 76.7% |
| | Spanish General Election 2004 | 75.7% |
| | Russian Presidential Election 2004 | 71.2% |
| | UK General Election 2005 | 61.3% |
| | Mexican Presidential Election 2006 | 58.6% |

### ? Questions ?

1 Today, fewer people vote in UK elections than in the past. Try to suggest one effect or consequence of this.

2 What reasons can you suggest why fewer people are voting in elections?

## A fight for equality

It took almost 80 years of campaigning for women to be given the same voting rights as men. Many people (both men and women) believed that voting and government were safer in the hands of men than women. Faced with this kind of resistance, some groups of women began to campaign for women's rights in a more militant and violent way.

One of the most famous of these campaigners was Emily Davison, who was imprisoned several times for taking part in violent demonstrations for votes for women. Her sentences included one month for breaking windows in the House of Commons, and ten days for assaulting a man she mistook for the Prime Minister, David Lloyd George.

Eventually, Emily chose to give her own life to the campaign. In prison she attempted suicide by going on hunger strike and, on one occasion, jumping from an upper landing. In June 1913, she threw herself in front of the King's horse at the Epsom Derby, and died from her injuries.

3 'Anyone with a right to vote should always use it.' What are the arguments for and against this point of view?

## Compulsory voting

In 2003, Neil Kinnock, former leader of the Labour Party, described the low election turnout as a 'crisis point', and backed the idea of making voting compulsory.

Voting is compulsory in a number of other countries, including Australia and Belgium, where recent election turnout was well over 90 per cent.

## Fines and penalties

Voting has been compulsory in Australia since 1924. The penalty for people who fail to turn up to vote, without good reason, is a fine of $50 (about £20). In Belgium a similar fine is imposed, although a person who repeatedly refuses to vote may eventually be sent to prison.

However, the phrase 'compulsory voting' is not quite accurate, as people are required only to enter the polling booth where they cast their vote. They do not have to vote. Some choose to leave their voting paper blank.

**4** Put the four statements below in the order in which you agree with them. Place the statement that you most agree with first.

   **a** 'It would be wrong to make people vote. Voting is something that people should decide to do for themselves.'

   **b** 'How can a politician claim to win an election if most people didn't take part?'

   **c** 'Making people vote will not deal with the basic reasons why so few people are interested in elections.'

   **d** 'Compulsory voting is the only certain way of increasing voter turnout.'

**5** Are you in favour of or against introducing some form of compulsory voting? Give reasons for your answer.

## KeyWords

### European election

Elections for members of the European Parliament (in Strasbourg, France), which take place every four years.

# Local government

This unit looks at some of the responsibilities of local councils and asks whether they should be given more powers.

## Standing for the council

### Just William

At the beginning of 2007, the age at which a person could stand for election to their local council was lowered from 21 to 18 years of age.

In the local elections later in the year, several 18 year olds stood for election. The youngest was William Lloyd, a student at school in Brentwood, Essex, who beat off Liberal Democrat opposition to become Britain's youngest councillor. He had worked as a volunteer for the local Conservative Party for two years, and stood for election while he was still studying for his A levels.

### ❓ Questions

**1** What are the advantages and disadvantages of having a young person such as William as a local councillor?

**2** Some people say 18 year olds are too young to stand for election. How far would you agree?

## Local councils

The way in which local councils in England and Wales are organised can seem very complicated, especially because of all the different names that are used: parish councils, district councils, county councils, metropolitan, and borough councils.

The council arrangements in your area will largely depend on whether you live in a village, a small town, a large town or a city.

If you live in a village or small town, you will probably have a parish council, a district council and a county council; and the various services you receive will be supplied by these three different groups.

If you live in a large town or city, you will probably be part of just one borough or metropolitan council. These councils tend to be responsible for all the local services.

## What do councils do?

*Parish councils* look after public areas in a village, such as litter bins, lighting, ponds and the village hall.

*District councils* commonly have a responsibility for housing, leisure centres and refuse collection.

*County councils* provide the remaining services, such as education, libraries, planning and roads, and they take responsibility for the development of the whole area.

*Borough or Metropolitan District Councils* provide people in their area with all of the above services. They are sometimes called unitary authorities because the services are provided by one organisation.

## Where do councils get their money from?

About a quarter of the money spent by councils comes from **council tax** and rent. Councils also get money from the local tax (known as rates) paid by businesses and from government grants.

Special formulae are used to decide how much money councils receive from government. These take into account the number of people living in the area and try to make sure that poor areas are given a fair share of cash.

## Local or national?

### More local

In October 2007, an official report was issued into an outbreak of serious infection that took place in three hospitals in Kent. Over a period of 18 months, more than 1,000 patients who attended the hospitals picked up a serious infection – from which 90 people are thought to have died.

Soon afterwards, the person in charge of the hospitals resigned, taking full responsibility for his part in what happened. However, he also said that the events would have been less likely to occur if more decisions about running the hospitals could have been taken at a local, rather than national level, stating that the National Health Service is far too centralised.

Today, this is a big question in politics in Britain. Should more decisions be taken at a local level? Would this be more, or less fair? There are arguments on both sides.

3 In 2005, hunting with dogs was banned throughout England and Wales. Imagine that an opinion poll found that most people in one particular region, for example the south west, were against the ban. Would it be right to allow hunting to begin again in this area?

4 What arguments can you think of in favour of more decisions being taken locally? What are the arguments against?

## KeyWords

### Council tax

A local tax paid by householders, based on the value of their property in 1991 (or 2003 in Wales).

# Devolution

This unit looks at some of the effects of the arrangements for government in Wales and Scotland.

## Going it alone

### Free prescriptions

In 2007, members of the National Assembly for Wales in Cardiff voted **unanimously** to abolish all prescription charges. This allows people in Wales to get medicines prescribed by their doctor free of charge.

The government in Scotland has similar plans, which will come into force by 2011. However, most people in England will continue to pay for their prescriptions, at a cost of around £7 a time.

This is an example of how life can vary in different parts of Britain – differences that will probably continue to grow in the future.

## Self-government

### More local

In 1997, people in Wales and in Scotland took part in a **referendum** to decide whether each nation should have greater control over its own affairs. This is called **devolution**.
In Wales, people narrowly voted in favour of a Welsh Assembly. The vote for a parliament in Scotland was much stronger. Two years later – in 1999 – the National Assembly for Wales and the Scottish Parliament were opened. Until this time, both countries had been largely governed from London.

## ? Questions

1   How much do you think it matters if prescriptions are free in some parts of the United Kingdom, but not in others?

2   Some people believe that Great Britain should eventually be split into separate states. But many disagree. Draw up a list of the possible effects of separating England, Scotland and Wales.

## Powers

Today, the Scottish Parliament can pass laws on many areas of life, including: education, health, housing, the police and the justice system. Some matters, however, still remain under the control of the UK Parliament in London. These include defence, foreign policy, social security, the law at work – and matters like abortion and gambling.

The National Assembly for Wales has fewer powers, but can pass its own laws on education, health, housing and social services.

There is also an Assembly in Northern Ireland – at Stormont, on the outskirts of Belfast. This too has powers to decide on education, agriculture, health and the environment.

## Change

In many ways, life in various parts of the UK is very similar – although there are important differences in culture and tradition. However, since 1999, decisions taken by the Welsh Assembly and Scottish Parliament have brought further differences between life in England, Scotland and Wales.

## In Scotland

- all elderly people can receive free personal care
- anyone over 65 without central heating in their home can have it installed free of charge
- students at university do not have to pay tuition fees
- under Scotland's legal system (which has always been different from England's) children can be charged with a crime from the age of eight, and can see a doctor alone from the age of 12.

## In Wales

- there is a different education system from England and no national tests for seven-year-olds
- students pay lower university fees than those in England
- there are no prescription charges.

PRESCRIPTIONS

£000

NATIONAL TESTS

3 On balance, are you in favour of or against devolution? How far would you go in separating England, Scotland and Wales?

## The words we use

The **United Kingdom** consists of four countries: England, Scotland, Wales and Northern Ireland. **Britain** or **Great Britain** refers only to England, Scotland and Wales. The **British Isles** describes Great Britain, Ireland and Northern Ireland, plus all the islands around our shores, including the Isle of Man and the Channel Islands.

## A very short history of Great Britain

*England, Scotland and Wales were originally made up of a number of small separate kingdoms. However, after the Norman invasion in 1066, most of Wales came under English control (although many in Wales opposed this), but Scotland remained independent, with its own parliament. In 1603, Scotland and England shared the same king – but the countries did not unite until 1707, when England put pressure on Scotland to unite and the two kingdoms became one.*

## KeyWords

### Devolution
Transferring power from central government to the UK's nations.

### Referendum
A vote in which people are asked to accept or reject a particular proposal.

### Unanimous
Complete agreement.

# The European Union

This unit outlines some of the things that the European Union tries to do, and asks you to explain what you think about its aims and purposes.

## Origins

Berlin after the siege in 1945.

At the end of the Second World War in 1945, governments throughout Europe were determined not to repeat the horrors of the War in which 50 million people had died. Germany and France had been at war three times in the previous 80 years.

In 1951, six nations – France, Belgium, Italy, Luxembourg, the Netherlands and West Germany – began to co-operate together in the production of coal and steel.

In 1957, the same six countries agreed to make trade easier by cutting **customs duties and tariffs**, and formed what became known as the European Economic Community. Other countries, including Britain, saw the advantages of this and joined later in 1973.

In 1993, new agreements bound the countries closer together, giving rise to what has become known as the European Union (EU). In 2007, two more countries joined the EU. There are now 27 **member states**.

## What does the European Union do?

One of the main purposes of the European Union is to allow people, goods and services to move freely between member states. This is known as the creation of a single market. A large market such as this makes it easier to sell goods to other countries.

## Trade

Over the last 30 years, member states have agreed all kinds of measures to improve trade between themselves. A number of EU states also share the same currency, the Euro.

## Other changes

Creating a single market has meant that certain laws, rules and regulations have become the same throughout all member states. These particularly apply to laws about employment, health and safety, and the environment. For example, no EU state is allowed to have laws that unfairly discriminate against someone because of their sex, race or ethnic group.

## Work

EU citizens are entitled to work in any EU state, and should generally be offered employment under the same conditions as citizens of that state.

## Travel

Citizens of EU member states have the right to travel to any other EU country, as long as they have a valid passport or identity card.

## Residence

EU citizens have the right to settle in any member state and, in general, to enjoy the same rights as other people living in that country.

## ? Questions

1 Since it has been in existence, the European Union has tried to:

- reduce the chances of war in Europe

- increase trade and wealth in Europe

- allow EU citizens to move easily from one European country to another

- allow EU citizens to work wherever they choose in Europe

- improve the environment in Europe.

a Do you disagree with any of these aims? If so, explain why.

b Can you see any risks associated with any of these aims? If so, try to explain what they are.

## KeyWords

**Customs duties and tariffs**
Taxes paid on goods that come in from one country to another.

**Member state**
A country that is part of the EU.

# The European Union

## Reporting Europe

For many years, stories have appeared in British papers reporting new regulations and laws produced by the European Union. Examples include EU demands that rhubarb and cucumbers must be straight and not excessively curved, an announcement that double-decker buses could be banned, as could smoky bacon crisps, and the right to buy a bone for your dog from the butcher.

## MYTHS AND LEGENDS

News on the European Union is sometimes misreported in the British press.

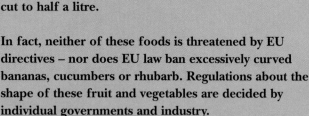

### Bread, milk and bananas

In 2006, *The Times* reported that the British 'pinta' and the traditional sliced loaf were being threatened by new EU legislation. Bread, the report stated, would be required to be sold in standard EU sizes, and the pint of milk would be cut to half a litre.

In fact, neither of these foods is threatened by EU directives – nor does EU law ban excessively curved bananas, cucumbers or rhubarb. Regulations about the shape of these fruit and vegetables are decided by individual governments and industry.

## Why does this happen?

None of these stories is true, but they do raise the question of why articles like these appear so often in our newspapers, often under headlines like 'Barmy Brussels'.

### ? Questions

1 Three reasons why newspapers might report EU news inaccurately are as follows.

- It is difficult for reporters to be completely accurate because EU rules are so complicated.

- The journalists are just trying to be entertaining.

- Some newspapers are very critical of the EU, and deliberately distort some of the stories that they report.

Which, if any, of these explanations do you think are correct? Try to give one reason to support your view.

## Britain and the EU

The origins of the European Union go back to the early 1950s when France, Germany, Belgium, Italy, Luxembourg and the Netherlands created an economic community that would bind the nations together and reduce the chances of another war. The British government of the time was reluctant to join, but its attitude began to change by the early

1960s when it became clear that British trade and influence would benefit from membership. However, Britain's application to join the European Community was twice rejected by the French Prime Minister of the time, and it wasn't until 1973 that Britain became a member.

In 1975, people in Britain had the opportunity to vote on whether the country should stay in or leave the community. By a majority of 2:1, people voted to stay in the European Community. Despite this vote of confidence, debate about Britain's membership of the EU has continued for the last 30 years.

## Where do you stand?

Here are some things that people have said about Britain's membership of the European Union.

**Amy:**
'So much of our trade is with the European Union that everyone's standard of living in this country would fall if we left the EU.'

**Henry:**
'The trouble with Europe is that ordinary people don't have enough say in what goes on. It's all too remote.'

**Louis:**
'Towns and cities throughout Britain benefit from money from the EU.'

**Marie:**
'Britain did not fight two World Wars to be governed by bureaucrats in Brussels.'

**Paul:**
'The EU means that the countries of Europe will never be at war with each other.'

**Simone:**
'I am worried that people from all over the EU can come here and take our jobs.'

**Theresa:**
'I like the idea of being able to travel to and work in other EU countries so easily.'

**Victor:**
'Some of the EU's policies have damaged this country. Take fishing, for example. So many fishermen have lost their livelihoods.'

2 Are there any statements in the text above that you disagree with? Explain why.

3 Which three statements do you most agree with?

4 Which of the following situations would you most welcome? Explain why.

- **As we were** Britain becomes independent and separate from Europe.
- **A trading partner** Britain has close trade links with Europe, but in other ways is completely independent.
- **As we are** Britain's relationship with Europe remains as it is today.
- **Closer links** European member states work more and more closely together.

# Migration

This unit looks at the history of migration to Britain and at some of its effects.

## A nation of migrants

If we go back far enough in time, almost everyone in Britain has their origins elsewhere. We are a nation of **immigrants** – with roots in countries throughout Europe, Russia, the Middle East, Africa, Asia and the Caribbean.

But Britain is also a country that people have left. Large numbers have moved away from Britain as **emigrants** to settle in places like Africa, Australia, Canada and the United States. Between 1850 and 1900, five and a half million people emigrated from England, Scotland and Wales.

A busy market in London. ▲

## Arrivals and departures

**Howard** was born in Essex and, when he left school, trained as a bricklayer. He worked on building sites in the south east for several years, but never really found the jobs and the money that he hoped for.

Howard had a cousin in Sydney, who told him about opportunities in Australia. Life out there sounded good – and a lot better than in England. Howard decided to take a chance. He left his job in Essex and went to stay with his cousin. Within a month, he found work.

Ten years later, and with a building business of his own, Howard decided that his future was in Sydney, and applied for Australian citizenship.

###  Questions

1 Read the stories on these pages, and explain why you think each person left their country. Are there any other reasons why people migrate?

2 What kinds of difficulties do you think each person probably faced in settling down in their new country?

3 What might make you migrate to another country?

**Henry** worked in the police canteen in Kingston, Jamaica. He liked his job, but read that British Railways was looking for people to work on the railway in England. The money was a lot better than he was earning in Jamaica, he thought the move could be a new start.

It was the late 1950s, and there was a great shortage of workers in Britain. Organisations like British Railways, London Transport and the National Health Service were offering work to people from overseas – particularly the Caribbean.

Henry applied to be a train guard. He took a test, had an interview and medical and was offered the job. He took out a loan to pay his fare to England, and arrived in London on a damp evening in 1960. To his surprise, Henry was given the dirty and dangerous job of coupling and uncoupling wagons. He never did work as a guard.

**Elma** was born in Bosnia, and is a hospital doctor. She is Muslim, like most people in her city; although some of her family and many of her patients belong to other faiths and cultures.

Until about 1990, the different religious and cultural groups in Bosnia lived peacefully together. However, by 1992, each of the main groups – Muslims, Serbs and Croats – wanted the country to move in a different direction. They could not agree, and fighting broke out. Many lives were lost, as each group tried to remove or kill people from other groups who lived in their area. (This is known as ethnic cleansing.)

At first, Elma did not believe that she was in danger; but started to worry about her safety when other Muslims were attacked. One day in 1994, she treated a Muslim woman and her daughter who had both been repeatedly raped by Bosnian soldiers. Elma knew that she and her daughter should leave. They packed two suitcases and headed for the border. They eventually reached England and claimed **political asylum**. When the war in Bosnia ended in 1995, about 250,000 people had been killed.

## Fear

Although some newcomers are welcomed when they move to a new country, migrants often – at least at first – face discrimination. As far back as 1440, the English parliament passed a law requiring all outsiders to pay extra taxes.

**4** What different kinds of emotions do people have when migrants arrive in their community? (These can be positive and negative.)

**5** Select one item from your list and try to explain why these views may be held.

# Key**Words**

### Emigrant
A person who leaves their region or country and settles elsewhere.

### Immigrant
A person arriving from another region or country.

### Political asylum
Protection from persecution, usually for reasons of race, religion or nationality.

# Migration

## Migration to Britain

### Invasion

People began to settle in Britain in around 5000 BC, travelling here from other parts of Europe. From 55 BC Roman soldiers, and later settlers, started to arrive from Italy, as the Roman Empire extended further north and west.

For the next 500 years, England was invaded and settled by the Jutes, Angles, Saxons and Vikings who came mainly from what are today the countries of Denmark, Germany and Norway.

In 1066, the Normans sailed from France and defeated King Harold of England at the Battle of Hastings. Over the next two hundred years Norman occupation of England and Wales brought new systems of government and law. French became the official language, and many French words of this period continue to be used today.

### Safety

Britain has a long history of giving safety (today known as political asylum) to people facing danger in their own country.

In the sixteenth and seventeenth centuries, Protestants from France came to Britain to escape religious persecution.

Between 1880 and 1910, large numbers of Jewish people came to Britain from what are now Poland, Ukraine and Belarus, fleeing the violence they faced at home. In the 1930s and 1940s, a smaller number of refugees came from Germany and central Europe to escape the Nazi Holocaust.

Since the 1970s, people have come to Britain from countries in Africa, southern Europe and the Middle East, and from Vietnam, trying to escape war and persecution.

### Quality of life

In recent years, many people have moved to Britain hoping to earn more money and obtain a better standard of living.

Britain's membership of the European Union allows people from other EU states to come to live and work (or study) in this country. (The same freedom is available to British people to live and work in other parts of Europe.)

People who live in countries *outside* the EU generally need to apply for permission to stay in the UK.

### ? Questions

1 Migration is sometimes described in terms of pressures or forces that *push* people away from their own country and *pull* them towards another. Using the above information name something that a) pushes people away from their country and b) that pulls them towards another.

# Migration control

## Benefit

It is generally agreed that migration to Britain brings a number of benefits. For example, without migrants certain organisations and businesses would find it very difficult to operate. Hospitals, transport, farming, cleaning and catering all rely on people who have come to Britain from overseas.

## Pressure

There is now some concern that the population of Britain is becoming too large and growing too fast. It is estimated that, over the next ten years, the number will rise by almost four-and-a-half million people. At present rates, about half this increase (just over two million) will be due to migration.

It is also believed that, at the moment, we do not have the number of houses, schools and hospitals required by a growing population. There are reports that this is producing difficulties in some areas. The government has to decide what to do.

2 The movement of people around the world has increased greatly over the last 30 years.

   a Draw up a list of some of the effects of migration.

   b Sort these out into positive and negative effects.

   c Take two of the effects, and explain why you have put them in the category that you did.

3 Look at the proposals below and try to write down at least one advantage and one disadvantage for each.

4 What would you suggest the government should do? Try to give reasons for your answer.

## Answers?

Here are some ideas that have been suggested:

- Do nothing and allow the population to rise or fall naturally.

- Smaller families – encourage couples to stop at two children.

- Restrict almost all immigration – and allow in only those who face serious danger in their home country.

- Place a limit each year on the numbers allowed to come and stay in Britain.

- Pick and choose, so that the only people who can stay will be those who are economically useful to the country, or face persecution at home.

- Encourage people to leave Britain – and live elsewhere.

# Race

This unit looks at racism and asks what behaviour should and should not be defined as racist.

## What is race?

The word race is used to describe groups of people who share common features, like hair type and skin colour.

However, today, scientists know that there is no significant difference between the genetic make-up of different 'races'. In fact, there are greater genetic differences between men and women of the same colour than there are between men or women of different races.

This suggests that race is an idea more based on human imagination than scientific fact.

## Racism

**Flora** is aged 81 and still doesn't like the Germans after her fiancé was killed in the Second World War. Flora never got over his death and has never married.

**Jenny** is English and has many friends from ethnic minorities. She finds them as pleasant and kind as people anywhere. She can't stand people who are racially prejudiced, but

does find it hard to like Americans. She thinks they have too much money and hates the fact that American companies have so much influence throughout the world.

**Ahmed** is from an Asian background and lives with his family in a small town in Lancashire. He runs a corner shop, but has repeatedly suffered

thefts, broken windows and all kinds of damage. He has started to hate some of the white people in his town.

**Jo** believes that people who come to live in the UK should adopt British customs and dress, and not stick to those of their former country. She is afraid the British will lose their culture.

However, she keeps quiet about these views and does not agree with people who attack immigrants.

**Owen** is Welsh. He wants home rule for Wales and thinks Welsh should be the main language in all Welsh schools. He also thinks there should be a law saying that no homes should be sold to English people

unless they work full-time in Wales.

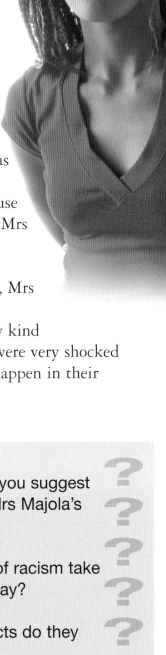

## Race hate

At 1a.m. on Saturday, Samora Majola and her four-year-old daughter were woken by the sound of a brick crashing through the front room window of her home in a small town just outside Belfast.

Mrs Majola, who came to the UK from South Africa a year ago, works as a care assistant. Shortly afterwards the nearby house of an Indian colleague of Mrs Majola was also targeted.

Speaking after the attack, Mrs Majola said that all her neighbours had been very kind and helpful, and people were very shocked that such a thing could happen in their community.

## ? Questions

1  Read the stories on page 54 and decide whether you think each person's attitudes are what you would call 'racist'. Explain your answer.

2  Imagine a line drawn across the page. On the left-hand side is 'not racist at all' and on the right-hand side is 'very racist'. Where would you place these different people and why?

3  Do you, personally, have any sympathy towards any of the stories on page 54? Explain your answer.

## Complicated

The people on the previous page are not real but they could easily be. If you think about the different kinds of feelings they have about people of different nationalities or colour, you can see that it is difficult to talk about racism as a single thing. You might have said that all these people are at least a bit racist but you might understand why some of them have these views.

Some people might find this question uncomfortable because it suggests that not all forms of racism are equally wrong.

4  What reasons can you suggest for the attack on Mrs Majola's house?

5  What other forms of racism take place in Britain today?

6  What kinds of effects do they have?

7  What reasons can you suggest that help to explain why racism occurs?

# Racial discrimination

## A new start

Bethan was unhappy in her job. One day she saw an advert in the paper for a receptionist at a local garage in the car and van rental department. It seemed ideal – good pay, easy to reach and a nice working environment. She would also have the use of a company car.

Bethan applied for the job and was called for interview. The interview went well and soon afterwards she was offered the job.

A fortnight later, Bethan started work. For the first couple of days she worked with Martin. He showed her how to deal with enquiries and prepare the papers for customers to sign when they rent a car.

'By the way,' said Martin on the second day, 'If you get a call from someone who is black or Asian, say that we haven't got any vehicles available. You've got to be careful who you lend cars to,' Martin continued. 'You can usually tell who they are or what they are like by the sound of their voice.'

At the end of the day the manager, Mr Deakin, came into the office. 'Martin, did you tell Bethan about our policy towards ethnic minority customers?' he asked.

'Yes, Mr Deakin,' Martin replied. 'No problem at all.'

Bethan said nothing, but that night went home feeling very confused.

## ? Questions

1 What would you advise Bethan to do, and why? Here are some ideas. She could:

- follow Martin's instructions, and not let vehicles out to black or Asian customers

- tell Mr Deakin that he was being unfair and should change the rules

- say nothing, but start looking for another job

- leave work immediately

- ignore Mr Deakin's rule and hope that he would eventually realise that black and Asian customers were no different from any others.

## Driven out

Bethan did not return to work. The next day she rang Mr Deakin and said that she felt she could not do the job. She did not give the real reason for her resignation.

A few days later Bethan went to a **solicitor** and explained what had happened. The solicitor told Bethan that she might be able to take out a case for racial discrimination against the garage for which Mr Deakin worked.

After listening to all the evidence, the **employment tribunal** decided that the garage had broken the Race Relations Act, and that Bethan had been forced out of her job because of the very difficult position in which she had been placed.

2 Mr Deakin believed that the garage should be able to rent its vehicles to whoever it chooses. Is the law correct in trying to prevent him from doing this? Explain the reasons for your view.

3 Bethan left her job voluntarily. Should she receive any compensation for losing her job?

4 What action should be taken to try to make sure that the garage treats all its customers equally and fairly?

## The law

The Race Relations Act 1976 states that it is against the law to treat a person less favourably than others because of their race, colour, nationality or national or ethnic origin.

A person who believes that they have been racially discriminated against may take their case to an employment tribunal.

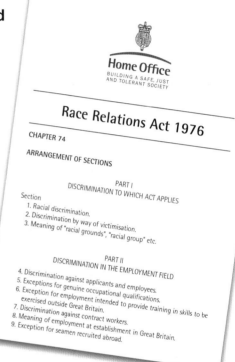

Home Office
BUILDING A SAFE, JUST AND TOLERANT SOCIETY

### Race Relations Act 1976

CHAPTER 74

ARRANGEMENT OF SECTIONS

PART I
DISCRIMINATION TO WHICH ACT APPLIES

Section
1. Racial discrimination.
2. Discrimination by way of victimisation.
3. Meaning of "racial grounds", "racial group" etc.

PART II
DISCRIMINATION IN THE EMPLOYMENT FIELD

4. Discrimination against applicants and employees.
5. Exceptions for genuine occupational qualifications.
6. Exception for employment intended to provide training in skills to be exercised outside Great Britain.
7. Discrimination against contract workers.
8. Meaning of employment at establishment in Great Britain.
9. Exception for seamen recruited abroad.

# Key**Words**

## Employment tribunal

A court of law that decides on employment disputes such as discrimination and unfair dismissal.

## Solicitor

A trained lawyer able to give advice and take action on a person's behalf over a range of legal issues.

# Personal identity

This unit looks at the nature of our personal identity and at some of the problems that may surround it.

## Who we are

If government plans go ahead, everyone in the UK who applies for a passport from 2010 will automatically be issued with an identity card, as well as their passport. Each card will contain 49 types of information, including the holder's photograph, their name, gender, address, place and date of birth, fingerprints, signature and details of their right to stay in Britain.

The information on the card will be unique; it will describe the card holder only, and no one else.

Although the details on each card should be accurate, they will not necessarily describe the holder's personal identity – that is, how they see themself. This is more complex. It may include many of the things on the card, but will contain other details such as values, beliefs, culture, interests and passions.

## ? Questions ?

1   Put down as many points as you wish to describe your personal identity – that is, how you see yourself.

2   Now try to pick out those points that you feel are most central, and explain why they are especially significant.

## Dual identity

In 1964, at the age of two, Imran arrived in England with his parents. His mother and father had both left good jobs in Pakistan to come to London, attracted by the British government's campaign to recruit people from Commonwealth countries to solve the labour shortage in Britain.

When Imran started school at the age of four, his life began to follow two separate paths. As the only black or Asian child in school, he was – at least in one way – different from everyone else. Although he gradually became aware of this, he joined in with all school activities, and did very well.

However, there were problems. Imran's parents were Muslim. At school he learnt about Jesus, but at home he learnt about Mohammed as well. Christmas could be difficult. Unlike other children, Imran couldn't talk about his presents, as he didn't really get any. Growing up had its difficulties too. Part of him wanted to mix with and go out with girls, just like most of his friends, but he didn't want to go against his religious upbringing.

# Identity problem

Sometimes a person's identity causes them difficulties due to the reactions of others. This happens particularly when the person or group is in a minority.

**Hugo**, aged 7, was wearing his England football shirt while playing on his scooter in an Edinburgh park during the 2006 World Cup. A man walked over to Hugo and hit him across the face, shouting anti-English abuse.

**Asif** feels that since the terrorist attacks by al-Qaeda in New York, Madrid and London, many people have a much narrower view of what it is to be Muslim. He believes that they see Muslims as a single group of people, opposed to the way in which people live in the West. In fact, Asif says, most Muslims in Britain have a great deal in common with everyone else – and only a very, very small minority share the views of those responsible for the attacks.

**Sarah**, aged 14, paid £10 to have her nose pierced. When she went to school the next day, the deputy head told her to remove the stud. Sarah did as she was told, but felt very disappointed. She felt that rules about uniform, jewellery and make-up stopped students from expressing their personality. 'I am a Goth,' she told her friend, 'but I can't show it because of the stupid rules. Teachers should not have the right to decide what kids do and don't do with their image – that's what makes us individual.'

3 During the early part of his life, Imran had two separate, but overlapping, identities – one with his family, and the other at school with his friends. Which path do you think Imran should have taken when he became an adult? What difficulties do you imagine he might have faced?

4 Are there any other situations in which people may have more than one identity? Explain why you think this might occur.

5 Hugo, Asif and Sarah all faced problems because of the way in which other people react to parts of their identity. What is your view about each case?

6 Sarah was not allowed to be a Goth in school. Are there any identities that you feel should not be shown or stated in public? If so, what are they, and why should they be banned?

7 Do you think young people sometimes have to adopt identities they are uncomfortable with?

# A national identity

This unit asks if we should celebrate our national identity and, if so, how.

## National day

On 1 August each year, Swiss people celebrate their national day. This is a national holiday with music, dancing, processions and fireworks in villages and towns all over the country. Switzerland has been a country in its own right since the thirteenth century, although four different languages are spoken. National day celebrates the signing of the treaty that created Switzerland in 1291.

## National pride

Many other countries have a national day – and often this is a public holiday. In Britain, this is generally not the case. Most large towns and cities in England have some sort of event to mark St George's Day (23 April), but it is rarely celebrated in schools or by individuals themselves, and hardly anyone wears a rose.

St George is recognised as a Muslim prophet as well as a Christian saint. He is also the patron saint of number of other countries and cities, including Georgia, Germany, Portugal, Palestine, Venice and Moscow.

St David's Day is of much more importance in Wales. On 1 March, many people wear a daffodil or leek (both symbols of Wales), and schools hold singing and dance festivals and competitions (known as *eisteddfods*), often with children wearing national costume.

St Patrick's Day is widely celebrated in Ireland and elsewhere, but St Andrew's Day is a much quieter affair in Scotland. Both are official holidays, although in Scotland employers are not required to give their staff the day off.

One reason why national identity seems stronger in Wales, Scotland and Ireland may be because they were dominated by England for so long. National pride is a way in which these nations have kept their identity and prevented the influence of England from becoming too strong.

## A day for Britain

Recently, government ministers have suggested that a national day is held for Britain as a whole, in which people would come together and celebrate the many achievements of the British people. This, they say, would help to create a sense of British identity and bind together what has become a very diverse society.

### ? Questions ?

1 How important is it for countries to have a national day? What are the strengths and weaknesses of the idea?

2 Would it be a good idea to have a *British* Day? Give reasons for your answer.

3 If a British Day is created, when should it be – and what kinds of events should take place?

# Showing the flag

The 2006 football World Cup is remembered by many people as a great success. Held in Germany, it was well organised, enthusiastically supported, and the games were good to watch. The German team did well too, losing only to Italy in the semi-final.

As Germany's side progressed through the early rounds of the competition, more and more flags began to appear throughout the country in support of the national team. This had never really happened before in Germany because, until recently, there tended to be strong associations between the German flag and the events of the Second World War. Many Germans had felt that the development of the wrong kind of national pride in the 1930s had led their country to wage war on others and to persecute millions of people.

In the past, there have also been difficulties with the English flag. Its use by certain individuals and organisations meant that for a while it became associated with white-only racism.

## Patriotism

Every morning at the start of school, children and young people throughout the United States pledge their allegiance to the American flag. The pledge was introduced in 1892 as a way of uniting the country after the civil war.

'I pledge allegiance to the flag of the United States of America, and to the Republic for which it stands, one Nation under God, indivisible, with liberty and justice for all.' ▶

The United States is not alone in encouraging young people to be **patriotic** – but sometimes these measures are unpopular. In 2006, 400 Japanese teachers won a legal case objecting to the requirement that they raise the flag and sing the national anthem. In 2007, the new French president faced strong objections from teachers when he suggested that a letter written during the Second World War by a young member of the French resistance should be read out at the start of the school year to teach children to be proud of being French.

4 In what circumstances do you think people in Britain are or should be patriotic?

5 Do schools have a responsibility to encourage young people to be patriotic? If so, how should they do it? Are there any dangers or difficulties associated with this?

6 Does patriotism matter? Try to explain your views.

## KeyWords

**Patriotic**
Devotion to one's country.

# Understanding human rights

In this unit you are asked to think about the nature of human rights and how they can affect our everyday lives.

## Coming from history

Peter Golinski today lives in Newcastle. He is in his 80s and came to England from Poland in 1947.

Peter was born in a small town in Poland, close to the border with Germany. In 1939, when Peter was 13, his life suddenly changed when German troops invaded Poland. The Polish army was quickly defeated and Peter's town was soon occupied. Peter still remembers watching from his room as German soldiers walked into houses to help themselves to anything that was there.

Life under German occupation was very difficult. As a Jew, Peter was not allowed to go to school, and his father could not carry out his normal work. Instead he had to work for the Germans – building roads, burying the dead – anything they wanted him to do. No one could leave the town without permission from the German authorities.

One morning Peter saw German soldiers dragging Jewish men from their houses, then kicking and beating them in the street. He watched in horror as he realised that one of them was his father, and another his cousin. The men were marched into the market place where they were kicked and clubbed with rifle butts, and then taken to the barracks where they were held overnight. Someone had opened fire on a German soldier and, assuming the culprit must be Jewish, the German commander had ordered all Jews to be rounded up and beaten until those responsible gave themselves up. The following day Peter's cousin was dead and his father badly injured. The person responsible for the shooting, it was later discovered, was Christian, not Jewish.

### Invasion

When Adolf Hitler became Chancellor (Prime Minister) of Germany in 1933, he wanted to make his country stronger. He tried to do this by creating a larger Germany – one that included all people of German descent, even those living outside Germany's borders. In 1938, he ordered the invasion of nearby Austria and, a year later, of Czechoslovakia, and then Poland.

### Persecution

The German economy was in a serious state of decline when Hitler came to power. Thousands of people were out of work. Hitler blamed Jews for this, and set about excluding, removing or killing all Jewish people in all countries under Germany's control.

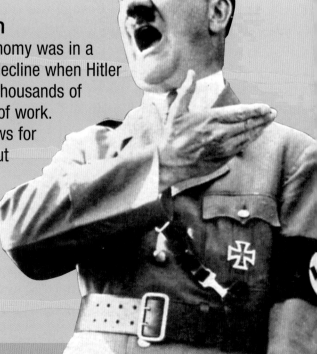

## ❓ Questions ❓❓❓❓

1 Look at the information on these pages, and try to draw up a list of the things that the Germans did in Poland that were wrong.

2 Select two or three items on your list and explain why they were wrong.

## Transportation

A few days later German troops arrived at the house to take Peter and his brother to the barracks. From there they were transported by train to a prisoner camp, and eventually to Auschwitz-Birkenau, a huge concentration camp that held about 400,000 prisoners. Although Peter himself survived, by the end of the war 210,000 people – largely Jewish and non-Jewish Poles, Gypsies and prisoners of war – had died there of starvation and abuse.

## Extermination

Auschwitz-Birkenau was also the site where other prisoners were taken for immediate execution. These were almost entirely Jewish people, transported from many parts of Europe. Over a period of three years, just under a million people, mostly Jews, were executed in the gas chambers at Auschwitz-Birkenau.

# The European Convention on Human Rights

At the end of the Second World War, many countries felt that something should be done to try to prevent similar atrocities from happening again.

A document was drawn up setting out basic **human rights** that governments who signed the agreement would promise to provide to everyone in their country.

This agreement is known as the European Convention on Human Rights. It has been signed by 45 countries throughout Europe.

The main rights under the Convention are the right to:
- life
- liberty and security
- a fair trial
- respect for private and family life, home and correspondence
- freedom of conscience, thought and religion
- freedom of speech
- freedom of peaceful assembly
- marry and start a family
- education
- free elections.

The Convention also forbids torture and slavery.

3 Look again at the account of Peter's early life. Which human rights under the European Convention did Peter and many other Poles lose during the Second World War?

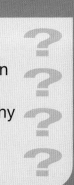

# Key**Words**

## Human rights
Basic rights that everyone is entitled to, which governments must protect.

# Human rights today

## The Human Rights Act

In 1998, Parliament agreed to make the European Convention on Human Rights part of UK law. The main reason for this was to protect ordinary people's human rights and to make sure that they were not treated unfairly by government or other official bodies.

The *Human Rights Act 1998* brought Britain into line with most other European states and many other countries worldwide, by having people's fundamental human rights guaranteed in writing and by law.

All British law must follow the rights listed in the Convention, and all public bodies – like the police, schools and hospitals – must carry out their work in a way that respects these basic human rights.

## How does the Act affect us?

Here are some situations in which the Human Rights Act could apply.

• **Interrogation** An explosion takes place, believed to have been caused by terrorists. The police are anxious to find those responsible. They arrest two suspects for questioning. Both refuse to speak. In the hope that the men will be persuaded to talk they are assaulted and threatened by the police and prevented from sleeping.

**EVIDENCE**

• **Evidence** The police are anxious to trap someone they suspect of dealing in large amounts of illegal drugs. They break into his house and install a secret listening device, which provides them with the evidence that they need.

• **Racism** A black woman is charged with theft. While listening to the evidence a juror hears another member of the jury make a racist comment about black people. The juror passes a note to the judge explaining what has happened. The judge allows the trial to continue.

• **Community work** The government announces a plan to require all 18 to 21-year-olds to complete a programme of voluntary service. Travel costs would be paid, but there would be no fee or wages.

## ? Questions ? ? ? ? ?

1  Use the information on page 63 to help you decide which rights are under threat in the situations above.

2  Now suggest what might happen if the Human Rights Act was applied in each situation.

# In court

A person who believes that their human rights have been broken may take their case to court. This can be a complicated process and judges often have to decide between strong arguments that exist on both sides.

## Uniform rights?

Shabina is Muslim and went to school in Bedfordshire. At the start of Year 9, she told the Head of Year that she would be wearing a *jilbab* dress to school. This is a long gown worn by some Muslim women that covers their arms and legs, but not their face and hands.

Until then Shabina, like many Muslim girls in her school, had worn trousers and a tunic, known as *shalwar kameez*. However, she believed that, from the age of 13, she should follow Muslim law, and cover her entire body in public, except for her hands and face.

Shabina's school, like many in Britain, had a strict uniform policy. It gave pupils the option of wearing trousers, skirts or the *shalwar kameez* – but not the *jilbab*. The school told Shabina that she could not attend lessons unless she wore the right uniform.

## No agreement

Over the next two years, neither side could reach agreement, and Shabina did not go to school. Eventually her lawyers applied to the High Court for a judge to decide on the matter.

Shabina's lawyers claimed that the school breached her human rights by not allowing her to wear traditional religious dress.

3 Look at the list of human rights on page 63. Which right or rights are relevant to this case?

4 What are the arguments in favour of Shabina being allowed to wear a jilbab to school? What are the arguments against this?

5 What are the arguments in favour of the school's decision not to allow Shabina to attend wearing a jilbab? What are the arguments against this?

6 The Court had to decide whether the school was breaking Shabina's human rights. What would your decision be? Give reasons for your answer.

# Universal rights?

## The death of James Bulger

In 1993, people all over Britain were shocked to hear of the death of two-year-old James Bulger. He was taken from a shopping centre by Robert Thompson and Jon Venables, who tortured and battered him and left him to die on a railway line. Thompson and Venables were ten years of age at the time.

The trial for the two boys, who were by then eleven years old, took place at Preston Crown Court, a court where adults are normally tried.

There was huge interest in the case throughout the country. Thompson and Venables were described in parts of the media as the most evil killers in living memory. The trial took place in a highly charged atmosphere. Later a member of the jury said that the boys were 'largely frightened and unaware of what was going on'.

After both boys had been found guilty, their lawyers claimed that the trial had been held in a way that broke human rights law. It was wrong, they said, for children to be tried in a similar way to adults. They said the case should have been held in a special juvenile court, well away from the public gaze. The judges at the European Court of Human Rights (below) agreed that Robert Thompson and Jon Venables did not receive a fair trial.

▲ The CCTV image of James and the two boys.

## In some, all, or every case?

When the European Convention on Human Rights was created it was decided that certain rights could not apply in every single situation. These exceptions are stated in the Convention.

The following exercise asks you to decide on some of those situations where you think human rights should not apply. You will need to refer to the list of human rights on page 67.

### ? Questions

1  Look at the list of human rights opposite and decide which article the judges decided had been broken in Robert Thompson's and Jon Venables' trial.

2  Why is it important to make sure that a trial is conducted fairly?

3 Draw two columns on your page. Read through each of the human rights below. In the left-hand column, list those rights that you think should apply in every single case – regardless of circumstances. In the right-hand column write down the remaining rights. These are those that you think might not apply in every case.

4 Take the rights you have listed in the right-hand column and, alongside each one, make a note of those circumstances in which you think it should not apply.

For example, if you thought a ban on torture (Article 3) should not apply in all circumstances, state when you think it might be acceptable for the police or military to torture suspects.

# UK law

**There are 16 basic human rights in the Human Rights Act, including:**

**Article 2** Everyone has a right to life, and the right to have their life protected by law.

**Article 3** No one shall be tortured or receive inhuman or degrading treatment.

**Article 4** No one shall be held in slavery or forced to work.

**Article 5** Everyone has the right to liberty and security.

**Article 6** Everyone who is charged with an offence is entitled to a fair trial, which should be in public, unless this would not be in the interests of justice.

**Article 7** No one may be punished for something that was not a crime when it was committed.

**Article 8** Everyone has a right to have their family, private life and correspondence respected.

**Article 9** Everyone has the right to freedom of thought, conscience and religion.

**Article 10** Everyone has the right to freedom of expression.

**Article 11** Everyone has the right to freedom of assembly and association.

**Article 12** Men and women of marriageable age have the right to marry and have a family.

**Protocol 1, article 1** Everyone has the right to peacefully enjoy their possessions.

**Protocol 1, article 2** Everyone has a right to education.

**Article 14** These rights should be available to all citizens, without discrimination.

# Index

# Cross-referenced key words